"[A] vibrant debut about sex workers in a Casablanca brothel."
—*New York Times Book Review*

"Startling...impressive...this tragic work remains timely and relevant, encouraging the reader to reflect on universal themes of gender norms, the self-perpetuating cycle of violence, and the inextricable ties that forever bind victims and their victimizers."

—*Washington Independent Review of Books*

"Written in elegiac prose that tends toward the poetic register of the ghazal, Mohamed Leftah's novel brings a specific place and time to an aching kind of life, even as it tells, with great empathy, the story of a people who are often relegated to the shadows. The relationship between Zapata and 'the Dane,' Nadia and Sophia, and the stories of Rose and Nectarine will stay with readers a long time. Fans of Anosh Irani's *The Parcel* and Orhan Pamuk's *My Name Is Red* are especially in for a treat." —Shastri Akella, author of *The Sea Elephants*

PRAISE FOR
Captain Ni'mat's Last Battle:

"Alluring...graphic and sensuous without being prurient, and a piquant exploration of masculinity, gender, societal taboos, and the nature of love." —*Publishers Weekly*

"Thought-provoking and engaging, with well-realized characters and a satisfying conclusion."   —*Booklist*

"Leftah is highly regarded in the francophone literary world ('An observer of the abyss. A champion of delight')... [*Captain Ni'mat's Last Battle* is] a stylish and intelligent read...a landmark statement in Egypt's exciting national conversation."
—*The Spectator*

"I read this gorgeous book in one sitting. The writing is poetic and breathtaking, rich with history. A must-read...*Captain Ni'mat's Last Battle* is so riveting!"
—Hasan Namir, Lambda Literary Award–winning author of *God in Pink*

"Hidden behind this novel, with its refined erotic writing style, is above all a highly subversive work."   —*Télérama*

ENDLESS FALL

Endless Fall

A LITTLE CHRONICLE

Mohamed Leftah

*Translated from the French
by Eleni Sikelianos*

*

OTHER PRESS
NEW YORK

Poetry excerpt on page 51 from "The Drunken Boat" ["Le Bateau ivre"] by
Arthur Rimbaud, 1871, adapted from a translation by Wallace Fowlie in
Complete Works, Selected Letters, The University of Chicago Press, 2005.

Production editor: Yvonne E. Cárdenas
Text designer: Patrice Sheridan
This book was set in Minion Pro by
Alpha Design & Composition of Pittsfield, NH

1 3 5 7 9 10 8 6 4 2

Library of Congress Cataloging-in-Publication Data
Names: Leftah, Mohamed, author. | Sikelianos, Eleni, translator.
Title: Endless fall : a little chronicle / Mohamed Leftah ; translated
from the French by Eleni Sikelianos.
Other titles: Chute infinie. English
Description: New York : Other Press, 2024. | "Originally published in
French as Une chute infinie in 2008 by Éditions de la Différence, Paris,
and reprinted in 2018 by La Croisée des Chemins, Casablanca"—
Title page verso.
Identifiers: LCCN 2023035506 (print) | LCCN 2023035507 (ebook) |
ISBN 9781635423020 (paperback ; acid-free paper) |
ISBN 9781635423037 (ebook)
Subjects: LCSH: Leftah, Mohamed—Fiction. | Suicide—Fiction. |
Toleration—Morocco—Settat—Fiction. | Settat (Morocco)—Fiction. |
LCGFT: Autobiographical fiction. | Novels.
Classification: LCC PQ3989.2.L427 C5913 2024 (print) |
LCC PQ3989.2.L427 (ebook) | DDC 843/.92—dc23/eng/20240220
LC record available at https://lccn.loc.gov/2023035506
LC ebook record available at https://lccn.loc.gov/2023035507

ENDLESS FALL

THE LETTER

*

"Dear Monsieur Ciccion,
   Please ask my mother to forgive me.
   I wish Nabil eternal happiness."

BY THE TIME MR. CICCION, HIS FACE WHITE AS A sheet and his hands trembling, would begin to read and try but fail to understand the meaning of the note, so clear, so limpid even in its reticence, the young man who had just written it would already be stretched out on the courtyard's clay ground.

...Stretched out...beneath the clouds...

Sweet scents don't tickle his nose;
He sleeps in the sun, a hand on his chest
Motionless...[1]

It is from memory and in memory of an unforgettable courtyard sleeper—a courtyard that, an instant
before it received the celestial, splendid body's fall, was
still dusty, and from that moment on became a princely
court—that I begin and dedicate this "little chronicle."[2]

Which opens no holiday in my days.

Pleasure or amusement, even less.

---

[1] Rimbaud, "The Sleeper of the Valley."
[2] I've borrowed this expression from the Italian writer Leonardo Scia-
sia, who gave this title to a group of tales and stories. In one of these
little chronicles, "Mata Hari in Palermo," he explains his approach:
"The small true facts of the past, which the chroniclers relay with im-
precision or reticence, and which historians neglect, sometimes open
in my hours and days something like a holiday. I mean that they become a vacation and amusement both, like reading an adventure book
or a detective novel."

NO MORE THAN A QUARTER OF AN HOUR HAD passed between the moment when I climbed the staircase with him to reach the fourth-floor classroom where Mr. Ciccion had already started his history class—we were both late—and the moment when he became this sleeper in the bloodied courtyard; a smiling sleeper in the valley.

Motionless...

More than forty years later, I still see all the stages, the unstoppable sequences of this transmutation, unfurling so clearly before my eyes.

Five.

Five sequences. Each one thoroughly defined, each thoroughly distinct.

Autonomous yet interdependent, as bound as the fingers on a hand.

The contours of a drama, in a form already outlined before it bursts into the world, so clearly sketched that for a long time the idea of this little chronicle seemed to me a kind of profanation or attack.

Against a face at once gymnast's and ballet dancer's, a face closed in on its own unsayable grace, its final and tragic beauty, its mortal perfection.

A face with no need of chronicler, narrator, nor celebrant to challenge, in its pure immateriality, the perverse work of time and oblivion.

SETTAT

*

AT THE TIME THESE EVENTS TAKE PLACE, THE time of the facts reported in this little chronicle, Settat was still nothing more than a tiny village dozing like a lizard under an unchanging blue, sunlit sky.

Two annual events startled it out of its lethargy: the faithful seasonal fires that lit up the *nouallas*, those thatch huts nestled on a hillside at the edge of town, which doggedly survived and rose from the ashes like phoenixes; then the unpredictable floods crashing out of Wadi Ben Moussa.

A burgeoning story, still in its first stuttering, but already common knowledge and as condemned as adultery...

A suicide...

PARDONING GESTURE

*

WOULD IT BE RIGHT TO TREAT HER AS AN ADUL-
terous woman, responsible for her son's suicide?

Khalid's mother had been a widow such a long
time. Her best years were burnt to ash by a dessicating
fidelity to the memory of her dead husband.

In his brief missive, the first person Khalid evoked
was this woman harried by the hounds of judgment.
In the last moments of his life he addressed his mother,
begging her to forgive him.

One of the most beautiful, moving gestures, rising from the depths of our geographical, psychic, and
cultural soil, is the one in which two people, in the
same movement and at the same time, give each other
chaste kisses on the head and on the hands. They
might be of different ages or sexes, of different social
standing or character, but in this gesture all their dis-
similarities and disagreements, even their hatred, if
there has been any, evaporates.

What remains is a gesture of reconciliation, a

pardoning of mutual offenses, incomprehension, and wrongs that each might have done the other.

I imagine, I am even certain of it without having witnessed it, that just a few moments beforehand, on that morning when I climbed the staircase with Khalid, this gesture flowered between him and his slandered mother, that woman hunted by gossip.

This invisible gesture accompanied him like a traveler's viaticum.

For his last journey.

SHIP

*

WE'RE CLIMBING THE STAIRS.

We're late. I'm hurrying, but he scales each step with an extreme, strange slowness. It's as if his sculptural, athletic body is caught in a swell. As if with each step his body, tossed by invisible waves, is tottering between peak and trough.

Perplexed, a little worried, I stop to watch his pitching movement.

His right arm is in a cast held horizontal by a band of white fabric tied at the neck, and it swings subtly at each step before falling back to his chest.

Laughable rudder, in white plaster, of a ship pitching toward its brief, final port of call.

OFF TRACK

*

ANOTHER STAIRCASE, FAR IN SPACE AND TIME from the one in Settat, at what was then the only high school in town.

A chair rises slowly, high into the air—every time I remember it, this is the first image that looms up—the chair rises in slow motion, so high its upturned legs almost touch the paneled vault of the ceiling, like four extra limbs extending from the policeman lifting it. An avenging Hindu divinity with multiple arms, a colossal Hercules dominating in all his height the Moroccan students occupying their own embassy in France, wedged in the stairwell and lustily pummeled by a police squad.

The four supernumerary hands wave slowly, like recently hatched and still-awkward pincers from some enormous insect in the middle of a metamorphosis that has just abruptly hit the imago stage.

Eyes bulging, face flushed, mouth ajar, the meta-morphosed police officer pants with rage, and hatred, and constricted, restrained *jouissance*. He purposefully takes his time, letting fear stir the entrails of the prey snared in his trap, the unspeakably pleasurable moment when his newborn pincers will swing down on the cranial domes that will then spurt scarlet blood in thin trickles or in geysers, hot and thrilling. Then the officer's panting will become less strangled, slower, and a treacherous and gratified torpor, as after an orgasm long held back, will sweep over and inundate him after the deflowering that his four extra members, like so many sex organs, will have savagely accomplished.

But for the moment the chair legs still oscillate under the ceiling's vault, though I can't remember from which direction those sylvan wings took flight and opened monstrously, that fantastical chair that instantly made itself part of the policeman's body, extending it, crowning it, high up under the vault of the ceiling, beginning to wobble now almost discreetly, unsustainably delaying the onset of the predictable, inevitable fall.

As soon as the course of that inevitability was set, before I saw the blood spurt from the skull of one of my friends—was he the secretary of our chapter?—I started to scream, or, more accurately, something animal and instinctive burst from my throat, without a sliver of thought or will intervening, a cry that could not be stopped: "No! No! No!" A panic-stricken, impotent denial.

Then, in my turn, I fell.

SHIP
(Continued)

*

THE SCULPTURAL BODY, PITCHING LIKE A SHIP, ended up docked at the same step of the stairs where I had stopped.

—What's wrong, Khalid, are you hurt?

I had hardly asked the question when I realized how stupid it was.

The face, of which I will try at the end of these items, these paragraphs (Med. Latin, *paragraphus*, Gr. *paragraphos*, "to write beside"), to express, scrap by scrap, the radiating beauty, was pallid, dirty, ravaged.

The lips I knew as pink, full, and dewy were swollen and had turned a purplish blue, almost black, from some unknown contusion or alchemy. The brown, warm eyes, usually twined like a ball of wool with rays of light, had become two black globes, two lightless chasms.

Just as we say "a pregnant woman," there was in front of me a face, a countenance for which I find no other qualifying word than this: pregnant.

Pregnant with its own death.

And I realize now, more than forty years later, that I've been carrying inside me all these years that face pregnant with its death without being conscious of it, like one of those women who, according to a belief still deeply held in the villages, carries a "sleeping" fetus in her belly for years. I carried that unforgettable sleeper in the valley inside myself.

PRAYER

*

O Lord, give each of us our own death:
give each of us a death born of our own life,
which knew love and lack.

For we are only rind and leaf
and the fruit at the center
is that large death each of us carries inside.

Rainer Maria Rilke
The Book of Poverty and Death

THE FRUITS OF EDEN

＊

FACING THE VILLA BELONGING TO WHAT WE then called the civil inspector towered and flourished Settat's most beautiful mulberry tree. It was like the tree of paradise, that mulberry, and its fruits were forbidden to the descendants of Adam and Eve, to natives like us. The civil inspector's eldest son considered it his private property and protected it against intrusion with more ferocity than a guard dog.

Yet one day I dared trespass into the forbidden flora and climbed up that tree and, hidden amidst its foliage, reveled in its paradisiacal fruits: mulberries of a violet that neared black, melting in the mouth, rich and succulent.

When I clambered down, stuffed and sated with these delights, I was hardly on the ground when I found myself facing two naked daggers pointed straight at me: the laughing and awe-inspiring blue eyes of the ferocious guard dog.

The handsome, golden teen put his hands haughtily on his hips and smiled at me, still slicing me with the unbearable blue splendor of his eyes. He was squeezed into a severe, immaculate tennis outfit: undershirt, shorts, espadrilles in snowy white. He stood there like a gymnast, a fanatic young crusader, and a dazzling morning flower.

I put my right hand to my lips, fingers pressed together, and began to kiss the tips, moving them back and forth clumsily. It's the pathetic, tragic, and age-old gesture by which, in the harsh and violent land where I first saw daylight, the helpless victim begs the executioner to spare him.

The young crusader's smile flowered wider, the flashing blades of his eyes went colder, then his right hand rose high, high into the pure-blue morning sky. He tilted his head and chest back slightly, but before his inescapable movement, with all the grace of a tennis player midserve, before the ball, the hand, could split the air and crash into the net of my cheek, my guts, in one dense, warm, foul lump, ejected the fruits of Eden.

OFF TRACK
(Continued)

*

THE POLICEMAN WITH THE HYBRID BODY, WITH his four supernumerary limbs, was now in front of me, his head and chest tilted back. I shrunk and shriveled to the ground, as if that could hold off the inevitable blow. But as the chair began to fall I fell with it, in the same movement and into a tiny instant of time, a time and space entirely unlike the one I was in. I had fallen, as if into an abyss, into my childhood. I found myself in a paradisical and forbidden tree, being scolded by a stunningly handsome magistrate. I thought I'd forgotten this ancient scene, but my body was endowed with its own memory. Before the chair crashed into me, it reacted in the same manner it had all those years ago. It reacted to looming violence by transforming it into fecal matter, which it ejected in one lump.

EL REY

✳

EL REY TOOK HIS PRESTIGIOUS NAME FROM A card in the game called *ronda*, the one that features a king mounted on a steed, his right hand holding a scepter and his head girded with a tiara. Of the variegated marginal fauna that enlivened the lethargy of life in Settat, El Rey was one of the most well known. His kingdom was that of games when he was sober and prison when he went on a *muzhik*'s bender and wanted to turn the town to fire and blood. His life was rigorously divided between these two slopes. No ephebus, no virgin, no ripe woman, honest or not, would ever penetrate it.

His body, though, was sumptuous, tattooed in tones of green and shadowy blue. A raised anchor was an invitation to go sailing, the magnificent open maw of a tiger a beckoning to leap in.

El Rey perished by drowning in the flower of youth during one of Wadi Ben Moussa's floods, that stream that divided Settat, cutting it in half from east to west. El Rey was on one of his famous benders that day, with two policemen chasing him. Drunk, over-estimating his own strength, he leapt into the muddy flow and made for what, unbeknownst to him, would be his last shore.

When the flood had receded the next day, they found his body at the top of one of the soft green hills that begin their wavy lines at the edge of town. He was completely straitjacketed in the mud except for his spattered face, which emerged smiling, as if El Rey were taunting his pursuers even in death. He who had been so chaste his whole life now evoked a hedonistic patrician rising from a Pompeii come back to life, taking a mud bath under a brilliant sun.

There was no one to sing Rimbaud's harrowing lullaby into this motionless patrician's ears, this young sleeper of the hills fixed in the mud:

Feet in the gladiolas, he sleeps. Smiling
the smile of a sick child, he takes a little doze.
Nature, rock him warmly...

El Rey perished by drowning (or was he suicided by society?) two or three weeks before Khalid's fatal plunge.

Let the threnody written in a language other than theirs, by that man "with feet of wind," gently cradle, warmly and forever, these two splendid adolescents cut down in the prime of life.

MR. CICCION, PUZZLED BY KHALID'S BEHAVIOR, obviously a thousand miles from history class, his face pallid and his eyes fixed on a notebook as if on the abyss, stops next to him and gently asks what's wrong.

Without a word, Khalid stands up, gives a weak smile, and moves slowly toward the door. He opens it, gathers speed in two dancing steps and leaps over the railing.

THE DIVER

Schoolyard of packed dirt.

Ocher colored.

Khalid stretched out on his left side, head resting on his arm.

A swimmer petrified midcrawl.

The right arm, just a few moments ago of white clay, now ocher, too, and stained with blood.

Khalid will not raise his torso or his hand for the alternating run of the swimmer's crawl.

His feet will no longer beat the water.

Nor his heart.

When he leapt over the railing, the image of a diver instantly flooded my mind. Before I realized that there was no water where he would be falling, that we were not at a pool but on the fourth floor of a school building.

Stunned along with everyone in class, I quickly understood that Khalid had dived—and with such ease!—into the sea of eternity.

NOW, ONLY NOW, AFTER DIGESTING THIS DRAMA, can I unfurl and exhibit its sequences.

I'd like the reader to think not so much of the cinematographic signification of "sequence" as of its liturgical meaning: "a rhythmic song extending the Alleluia…"

Only now can I reread the laconic note, follow Khalid from his seat to the classroom door, describe his body swaying before the railing giving onto the void.

Only now can I keep him company on the walk, the procession of a dazzling Muslim adolescent from the classroom door to the railing: from choir loft to ambo.

And finally that last prodigious leap, a swordfish erupting into the air, before disappearing forever.

"Dear Monsieur Ciccion…"

The recipient of Khalid's final message was the students' most beloved teacher.

More than a teacher, he called to mind an artist, an *artiste maudit* like those invented and made famous in nineteenth-century France.

A red beard honed to a point, eyes a washed-out blue, face emaciated and exceedingly pale, he unfurled the splendor and decadence of the Roman empire for the young teenaged Muslims in a country that had just achieved independence, in a voice wrecked by alcohol and tuberculosis.

The entire class listened in religious silence to what this spindle-shaped storyteller topped in a Basque beret told them, bundled up in a shapeless coat buttoned up wrong, inside of which his body would suddenly shiver from time to time, even in summer. The professor would distractedly unbutton then rebutton his coat, still wrong, his hands trembling with alcohol, extend a pitiful, guilty smile as if he were apologizing for the ruin and decadence of his own body, which he offered up to the students as spectacle twice a week.

Yet they adored this decadent professor, whose mind was rich with so many crumbling empires, so many bygone splendors, vain and bloody battles, and mummified and incomprehensible dialects. His kindness, his smiling despair, largely redeemed the alcoholic "vice" that was ruining his health.

That's why the surprise was so widespread and profound when the drama unfolded in his class.

KHALID IS SITTING ON ONE OF THE BENCHES IN the second or third row.

He has removed the white strip of cloth tied at his neck that was keeping his plastered right arm horizontal. He lays that arm on the table, mineralized, white, inert. With his left hand, Khalid visors his brow and looks at the blank page of his history notebook.

He is not taking notes.

He is far from Rome and its crazy emperors, its cruel circus games and orgies, its legionnaires and conquests. So far from any history, large or small.

He is staring at the white abyss that has hollowed out before his eyes, into the graph paper of his notebook. As if to ward off that abyss, Khalid begins to write his letter: "Dear Monsieur Ciccion..."

Why did he choose the *artiste maudit*, the historian of decadence, as the messenger of such a short testament? Was it the secret and terrible prescience of one who was about to put an end to his days, somehow knowing that the elected recipient would not survive him by long? Is that why he appointed him messenger of forgiveness and eternal happiness?

A PANTHER OF THE NILE

*

KHALID HAD CHOSEN A SICK, ALCOHOLIC teacher as messenger of his final vows and wishes, but it was the Arabic teacher who appointed himself as his obituarist.

This teacher, an Egyptian civil servant—it was the era where the charismatic image of a modern Pharaoh fascinated and enthralled the Arab world—was named for the Muslim month of fasting, Ramadan.

The irony of some appellations! Everything about this son and herald of the Nile contradicted his name.

Deep laugh. A dockworker's or a furniture mover's shoulders. Thick and bushy jet-black mustache. Full, moist lips: sensual. Pearly teeth made for sparkling when he smiled, for shredding when he bit into fruit or flesh. Perfectly poured into life, like a tiger or a panther.

Yes, he was a panther, this son of the Nile named for the month of fasting.

As for the alcoholic, intemperate, and decadent Mr. Ciccion, nothing would have better fit in describing his deepest truth than the title of that short story by Kafka, "A Hunger Artist."

THE OBITUARIST

*

THE VERY DAY AFTER KHALID'S SUICIDE, HIS classmates and all the other students still plunged in affliction saw with surprise the Egyptian teacher's beautiful handwriting, unmistakable among a thousand cursives, unfolding in rounding, nimble spirals on the blackboard attached to the wall next to the director's office. He had transcribed the Koranic verses that specify the fate promised to those who have ended their days by throwing themselves into the abyss. They will be condemned in the hereafter to repeat their suicidal gesture endlessly. And it will not be the welcoming, maternal earth that receives their bodies jettisoned into the void, but Gehenna's tongues of fire.

That was the eschatological, apocalyptic destiny that awaited Khalid.

The teacher with the beautiful handwriting hadn't found anything more appropriate to excerpt from the book that begins each sura with "In the name of God, most Gracious, most Merciful." He undoubtedly had no idea about Ibn Arabi's exegesis, which takes into account precisely that immutable, formulaic phrase by which all the Koran's suras begin, that which says that divine mercy is the cement that connects and nourishes the universe. He boldly added, over eight centuries ago, that perpetual punishment was at odds with this original encompassing and everlasting mercy.

Consequently, even the flames of Gehenna would become, in time, a fresh, salvaging breeze to those who had endured them.

No, the panther had not read Ibn Arabi, or Al-Hallaj, or Jalal ad-Din ar-Rumi... It had voraciously swallowed the book without taking the time to digest it, but it had such beautiful handwriting and couldn't pass up such a rare occasion to display it for everyone's admiring gaze.

BUT THE YOUNG, RADIANT ADOLESCENT WITH no retrial option had already responded to his eternal damnation with this simple appeal:

"I wish eternal happiness to…"

SCAVENGER?

✳

I CALLED THE HISTORY PROFESSOR A MESSEN-
ger, the Arabic professor an obituarist. What does that
make me, presenting myself as a chronicler and com-
memorator of a suicide?

Like those beetles that bury carrion and cadav-
ers so the female can lay her eggs in them, am I also
a kind of *Necrophorus* insect, exhuming a suicide's
corpse as excuse and justification for a chronicle?

How to take this "little chronicle"? As an act of
scavenging or, on the contrary, something aimed at
saving from oblivion the tragic destiny of a gorgeous
young man?

I linked these items and writings with scraps,
diversions and ruptures, rage and love, to dissolve a
rhetoric, a writing, a calligraphic shroud.

I want to take those powdery white figures written
that day on the blackboard that fell like an avalanche
on an already broken body, and scatter them to the
winds.

Up against the flowery rhetoric, the empty chatter of polemics and assonant, rhyming prose, I want to pause...

To invoke and magnify the elementary, the organic...

The venal.

FLOWERS OF EVIL?

*

Since I invoked the flowers of rhetoric...

"He" had a predilection for botany class, which was offered in the second or third year of high school.

At the time of his adolescence, in his hometown, Settat (whose first letter, you will note, is the same as the first letter of Sodom), those male flowers who liked to act like or who were led by violence or seduction to metamorphose into female flowers were not rare. It was with one of those flowers that he went one day to the great mosque, a place they knew all the corners of, especially where the men performed their ritual ablutions before prayer. They rushed into a bathroom and locked themselves in. His heart beating hard, the flower perfectly calm. She already knew the terrain, nauseating, but how rich and voluptuous!—this flower whose metamorphosis had been early. With precise, harmonious, and expert movements, she flared her corolla into full-golden cleft sphericity, in a position of total offering.

The lover of botany buried his sex in the pistil of vibrant flesh. He closed his eyes, so sweet, warm, and radiant was the night that seized him. When his pollen spurted for the first time into a flowering night, he moaned with pleasure and his knees began to tremble so violently that he wound his hands around the flared corolla as around a supporting bough so as not to sway and sink down.

The firm, friendly flower held him, and his fall was infinitely sweet, infinitely slow. He didn't even notice that he had pulled his pants back up. He asked the flower if she was ready to leave that marvelous and foul-smelling territory—brown, rigid turds were floating in the bowl like petrified sexes—but she indicated with an expressive gesture that she was going to offer herself a second pleasure, and immediately undertook that task. He left her to her comforts and exited the mosque toilets.

It wasn't until the next day that the older boys, already initiated, explained to him that what the flower was doing was masturbating, and the dilation he'd felt of his whole being, that slow, vertiginous fall into a night constellated with flowers, when his pollen spurted for the first time into the undifferentiated, yawning pistil of the world—that was called an orgasm.

THIS SEXUAL INITIATION IN A PLACE RESERVED for sewage, the toilets of the grand mosque, wasn't the most venal or profane act an adolescent of that era might be led to.

For those fiery, irrepressible youth who hit puberty early, a hypocritical and bigoted society allowed only corrupt or homosexual encounters.

If, as Goya claimed, the sleep of reason engenders monsters, sexual frustration leads to the flowering of monstrous love.

And our adolescent, now initiated, would one day have the occasion to know that bitter taste.

EROS AND THANATOS

*

The cemetery in Settat.

He and the neighbor's cleaning girl are walking among the immaculate, naked tombs, without even a single flower to cheer things up.

The maid lay belly down on one of the farthest graves, hidden from view. She was older than he was, maybe seventeen. She limped, and her armpits gave off a pestilent odor, her face was bereft of any notion of beauty, but she was named for a flower, the generic name for flowers in fact, Zahra.

He embraced and penetrated the deformed, graceless body, full of the divine because it was offered up in the open air, at any time, under the wide sky, to any ardent pubescent frustrated by his place in life. What happened next?

"He almost lost his balance and staggered. As he caught his footing, his head fell back, and the Milky Way flowed down inside him with a roar."

This is the fantastical image that closes the Japanese writer Yasunari Kawabata's novel *Snow Country*.

After this act of desecration, although he lifted his slightly constricted chest and his trembling knees, the blue sky without the slightest cloud that was their witness didn't roar at all, did not come down upon them like a tiger, did not light up the cemetery in flames, nor, why not?, the whole town of Sodom. The maid, the disgraced young girl with the generic flower name, took her time wiping between her cheeks with a scrawny tuft of weed, which she then tossed casually onto the helpless, stained, profaned tomb.

The blazing summer sky was just as blue, just as pure, and just as serene as ever.

A DOUBLE BEAUTY

*

Unforgettable
Loves
Flowering
In places of pestilence and death.
Funereal loves? Disgraceful? Venal?
Let them, by their very abomination, render the young man mown down in the flower of youth ever more royal, more splendid, purer and more untouchable.

Khalid was born to inspire wild love in a woman's body and soul.

At the same time, a secret femininity sometimes slowed his gestures or flashed in his eyes, those eyes like balls of brown wool twined with the sun's rays.

A proud, shimmering Saracen, Khalid had the beauty of a virile young gymnast, but also, by flickering turns, the unnerving beauty of those ephebi that antique Greek statuary immortalized in stone.

MISSING PAGES

＊

WHEN I DECIDED TO TAKE UP THIS "LITTLE chronicle" again, which wasn't called that but was simply a rough draft of a forgotten manuscript lost among others, I noticed that it was missing some pages.

I had no idea why, but I was certain of it. Among the missing pages must have been those in which appeared the gymnasts and ephebi of Greek antiquity—the first go at what would become this "little chronicle" was written the year the Olympic Games unfolded in Barcelona. It was the twenty-second modern Olympiad since the Baron de Coubertin had the brilliant idea of resuscitating the games, first celebrated in Olympia in the year 776 BC.

Should I signal it each time I notice missing pages? Try to recall and rewrite them? Or simply accept this interruption, this break, this incompleteness, even seeing it as a manifestation of the *hasard objectif* so dear to the surrealists, as if they marked Khalid's destiny with a seal?

A CONVULSIVE BEAUTY

*

AFTER HIS MOTHER, IT WAS NABIL KHALID thought of in the final instants he had left to live:

"I wish eternal happiness to..."

Nabil was the most talented left-winger the Settat senior team had ever known. His lightning dribbles and his corner kicks were as good as his driving shots; his intelligence in the game, really, was on everyone's lips and was constantly discussed.

But sometimes in the heat of action, his fans hanging on his every move, this soccer genius would suddenly stop, totter for an instant, then topple like a tree struck by lightning. A few spectators thought that for him to collapse like that, it must be because the other team's right-back, who stuck to his every move like glue, had tackled him savagely. They started to whistle and boo the beast. But those in the know, because they never missed a game, explained what had really happened. Already, two men with armbands were carrying a stretcher onto the field and running toward Nabil, his mouth foaming and eyes rolled back in the throes of a grand mal. Falling sickness.

THE MOST CHASTE OF KISSES

*

Khalid and Nabil.

The goalie and the left-winger.

The junior and the senior.

The younger and the elder.

A sculptural beauty, in complete balance and harmony, and a convulsive beauty. The attention, the concentration, the vigilant anticipation, and a breathtaking cavalcade ending in the throes of a grand mal.

We could continue with this inventory of polarities and oppositions, contrasting in parallel tracks. But to even begin to approach the burning heat of a friendship that inspired the younger man to write, on the threshold of death, that he wished eternal happiness to the elder who would survive him, we must, as always, turn to the imagination. Here, then...

To select the talented juniors who would become seniors, the coaches had organized a match between the two teams. So Khalid and Nabil find themselves, for ninety minutes, on opposite sides.

The referee has barely blown the whistle to start the match when Nabil, with his first ball, throws himself like an arrow, lands in the corner point, lifts his head to locate an unmarked teammate. But the first thing his eyes meet are those of the junior team's goalie, the youngest player on the field. Khalid's chest is snugly packed in a sweater the color of a flowering mimosa, and orange are the shorts that reach to his knees.

Nabil pauses and puts his hand up, visoring his forehead as if dazzled by the vivid colors. Before transmitting a parabolic flight pattern to the ball, he smiles at his friend, who like a feline ready to pounce, smiles back.

The spectators follow the ball's parabolic flight with their eyes, and the bird with multicolored plumage takes off.

Khalid falls on the packed earth, the ball nestled between his arms, and after two or three rolls to absorb the impact, he stands, the ball still held tight against his heart. Nabil and Khalid exchange conspiratorial smiles, which doesn't escape the spectators. They suspect they have just witnessed a secret, coded message being passed, and they are right to wonder.

Indeed, what was really exchanged across the parabolic trajectory? A ball? A smile? The most chaste of kisses?

As if mesmerized by the beauty of this secret ceremony, the spectators don't applaud until Khalid pulls them out of the enthralled spell by sending the ball deep into the opposing team.

ELEMENTARY PARTICLES

*

MODERN QUANTUM PHYSICS ALLOWS US TO burrow into a universe of elementary particles and their dazzling, vertiginous trajectories. To comprehend them and transform them into equations, physicists were obliged to endow them with taste, color, charm, and strangeness.

At the threshold of the intimate, ultimate structure of matter, near the secret beauty and terror nestled there, the only recourse was an appeal to the language of poetry.

A BEAUTY . . . THAT SAVES?

*

WITH A WORRYING CALM, KHALID HEADED FOR
the door. Not a single glance at any of his perplexed
classmates. His friend Widad, most fervent supporter
of the junior team goalkeeper, never forgave himself
for not having guessed the flight and outcome that
this slow, regal walk, superbly indifferent to the eyes
following it, was leading to.

As soon as he raced down the stairs with the rest
of the class and saw the swimmer frozen in midcrawl,
fully laid out on the ocher earth of the courtyard, he
was seized by the first epileptic fit of his life. From
that moment on, like the talented winger, Wadid lived
with the specter of these attacks. Epilepsy was an es-
sential, fateful sign in Khalid's life and would continue its vigilant watch beyond his death.

Beauty, grand mal, forgiveness of trespasses, suicide, compassion . . .

Could Khalid, in his short life, have encountered
Dostoevsky's dizzying universe? The author who one

day proclaimed that only beauty could save a world that had announced the death of God.

OUR SUBLUNARY WORLD

*

SADLY, EVEN BEAUTY, ON WHICH DOSTOEVSKY conferred redemptive powers, was, in our sublunary world, under the rule of generation and corruption, to use the language of the ancient Aristotelian philosophers.

Besides Khalid, there were two other junior boys who guarded the goal. The first was a Black athletic youth who brimmed with talent but who did with it as he pleased. He arrived one day on the field with his brain still smoke-fogged from kef, and forgot that he was supposed to stay between the posts. He frolicked among the other players once or twice, indulging in something that looked like a samba dance under the eyes of the stunned spectators, devastating the managers. They forgave him, but when he played the same game in the next match, the coaches let him know that they would henceforth take a pass on his dance performances. The second goalie was more serious, and they had high hopes for him. Indeed, he was tapped as goalkeeper after Khalid's suicide.

Years later, I chanced upon him one day in a bar in the center of Casablanca. If he hadn't addressed me, asking if I wasn't the nephew of Monsieur Abdel Hafid, his teacher the year of his certificate of studies, I wouldn't have recognized him. His hair had gone gray, he was missing several teeth, and he raised his glass with an alcoholic, trembling hand to toast: to the glorious days of Settat's junior team, he recalled wistfully, his eyes tearing up. A wreck, I don't know from what storm, had washed up at the foot of that counter.

And suddenly I saw again a bird of multicolored plumage in flight, an image that, as soon as it arose, gave way to that of a swordfish surging through the air for an instant, only to plunge one way, forever, into the sea of eternity.

But the beauty and perfection of Khalid's movement survived in its pure immateriality and—how can I put it?—redeemed the decay of the man toasting with me, who also in his youth had executed many a pure, winged, aerial leap of admirable beauty.

Perhaps Dostoevsky was not wrong after all.

OH, LET ME GO TO SEA!

✳

But yes, I have wept too much! Dawns are
    upsetting,
every moon is atrocious, every sun is bitter:
Acrid love has inflated me with an
    intoxicating stupor.
Oh, let my keel burst! Oh, let me go to sea!

In slang, "keel" means leg.

As you know, the author of "The Drunken Boat"
died in a hospital in Marseilles after they amputated
a gangrenous leg.

Khalid performed his own dive with one arm in
plaster.

Mineralized arm, gangrenous leg.

Fate's irony and cruelty for a dazzling goalkeeper,
and for a poet-seer whom we would come to call "the
man with feet of wind."

51

SWORDFISH

✳

THAT MINERALIZED HAND FORCED KHALID TO perform his dive in a singular manner.

Only his left arm was held in front, free and alive, like a swordfish's weapon, and with this extension in a flawlessly straight line his whole body lifted from the ground.

MORE MISSING PAGES

✳

WHEN I ARRIVED AT THIS POINT IN MY "LITTLE chronicle" I once again noticed missing pages, this time five or six.

What could I have written?—the draft was over a decade old—added again that during his flight as a swordfish splitting the air Khalid was in his last metamorphosis, his ultimate transmutation?

Yes, there was also that image of the sleeper in the valley laid out on his flank in an ocher-colored courtyard, but I had already sufficiently conjured that. So? For a long time I tried in vain to recollect what those missing pages I wrote in Paris, in the year of the twenty-second Olympiad, which took place in Barcelona, contained.

PRAYER

✳

TODAY, IN EGYPT, I DECIDED TO BRING THIS LIT-
tle chronicle to a close. In this region of the world torn
by conflicts and inexpiable hatreds, I think, dream-
ing, of that provisional truce that took place during
the Olympic Games, when the Greek cities ceased to
destroy each other in fratricidal wars and instead celebrated the games together.

Where did I actually write this? In Settat, Casablanca, Paris, Barcelona, Cairo?

We're at the site of Olympia, and it's the year 776
BC.

A sculptural adolescent, endowed with the beauty
of an ephebus, enters the Olympic pool deck slowly,
magisterially (I know, there was no swimming or diving competition in this period).

He has climbed the spiral stairs to the diving
board, at the top of which he stops for a moment or
two. His feet leave the board at last, and here he is, a
swordfish splitting the air; and this figure, immaterial,
closed-in in its perfect beauty, travels across centuries,

awaiting the scribe who will gather and vainly try to imagine it, resuscitate it, to give even the palest glimmer of it.

I wanted, in memory of my classmate who took his own life in front of our eyes, whom an Arabic professor buried in vengeful verses and to whom my society refused the prayer for the dead because he committed suicide, I wanted simply to raise this prayer for him, more than forty years later, the prayer that he was refused.

My hope is that the reader will accept this little chronicle as such and will have shared with me, for the brief time it takes to read, this prayer.

Cairo, July 2006

TRANSLATOR'S ACKNOWLEDGMENTS

✳

I WISH TO THANK DAVID RUFFEL FOR FIRST TELLING ME that I must read Leftah, and Omar Berrada, for so thoughtfully gifting me *Une chute infinie* over a decade ago, thinking there was some rhyme with my own family chronicles. Thanks are due also to Yvonne Cárdenas and her patience. A selection from this translation appeared in the 2016 "Crossing Boundaries: Morocco's Many Voices" edition of *Words Without Borders*, and gratitude is due to those editors too.

MOHAMED LEFTAH WAS A WRITER AND JOURNALIST BORN in Settat, Morocco, in 1946. He attended engineering school in Paris and then returned in 1972 to Morocco, where he became a literary critic for *Le Matin du Sahara* and *Le Temps du Maroc*. His novels include the critically acclaimed *Demoiselles of Numidia* (Other Press, 2023) and *Captain Ni'mat's Last Battle* (Other Press, 2022). He died of cancer in 2008.

ELENI SIKELIANOS IS A POET, WRITER, AND PROFESSOR OF Literary Arts at Brown University. Her work has been widely translated and anthologized, garnering numerous honors. Her books include *Your Kingdom*, *Make Yourself Happy*, and *The Book of Jon*.